ISBN 978-1-5282-0973-1
PIBN 10911559

English
Français
Deutsche
Italiano
Español
Português

www.forgottenbooks.com

Mythology Photography **Fiction**
Fishing Christianity **Art** Cooking
Essays Buddhism Freemasonry
Medicine **Biology** Music **Ancient
Egypt** Evolution Carpentry Physics
Dance Geology **Mathematics** Fitness
Shakespeare **Folklore** Yoga Marketing
Confidence Immortality Biographies
Poetry **Psychology** Witchcraft
Electronics Chemistry History **Law**
Accounting **Philosophy** Anthropology
Alchemy Drama Quantum Mechanics
Atheism Sexual Health **Ancient History**
Entrepreneurship Languages Sport
Paleontology Needlework Islam
Metaphysics Investment Archaeology
Parenting Statistics Criminology
Motivational

The AMPLE Project *

J.C. Boudreaux

Center for Manufacturing Engineering
National Bureau of Standards

1 Introduction

This report describes the Automated Manufacturing Programming Language Environment
(*AMPLE*) system, being developed within the Center for Manufacturing Engineering of the
National Bureau of Standards. The development of *AMPLE* is being undertaken for two
main reasons: to provide a precise mechanism for the construction of control interfaces to
industrial manufacturing processes; and to provide an integrated system of software tools
for translating product design and process planning specifications into verified equipment-
level control programs.

Work on the *AMPLE* project has been surrounded by a more comprehensive project
which investigates the design of advanced automated manufacturing systems. This project,
embodied in the Automated Manufacturing Research Facility (AMRF) of the National
Bureau of Standards, has provided an invaluable source of empirical data and practical
experience.

From the inception of the *AMPLE* project in October 1984, the design of the system
has been deliberately coupled with the development of rapid prototypes. There have been
two prototypes. The first was built during the initial design phase, and the second, now
being finished, is a more elaborately worked companion to Version 0.1. Both prototypes
have been built in FranzLISP, a popular dialect of LISP /10/. Since the LISP family is not
widely known in the world of manufacturing engineering, an appendix on this programming
language has been included in this report.

2 An Overview

All programming languages are based upon a model of computation and *AMPLE* is no
exception. Traditional programming languages, like FORTRAN, have *store-centered* models
of computation in which the interpretation of each feature of the language is reduced to
the behavior of an idealized von Neumann machine, and ultimately to the effect of that
behavior on the contents of store. However, the *AMPLE* model of computation is based
on the notion of *fully automated manufacturing workstations*, whose mathematical form,
though as yet imperfectly grapsed, is clearly much more complicated than that of any model
heretofore considered. The salient characteristic of this model is that success and failure
may only be determined by the occurrence or non-occurrence of certain preferred states in

---

*Certain commercial equipment and products are identified in this paper in order to adequately specify
the experimental procedure. Such identification does not imply recommendation or endorsement by the
National Bureau of Standards, nor does it imply that the equipment identified is necessarily the best
available for the purpose.

the physical universe, and thus is largely independent of such computer-related measures as side effects on store /6/.

An automated manufacturing workstation, also called a flexible manufacture system (*FMS*), is a hybrid manufacturing regime, having features in common with both manual manufacture and factory automation, while retaining its own definite characteristics. Though FMS systems differ in detail, there are sufficient uniformities for an accurate general picture to have emerged.

First, automated workstations are centered on a numerically controlled (NC) machines, such as horizontal or vertical mills, lathes, or coordinate-measuring machines. The phrase "NC" is intended to imply that all machining operations, especially those relative motions of the tool which modify part geometry or material condition, are performed under the direction of a user-defined program. Such programs are executed by an embedded computer, called the NC machine controller. NC part programs may be written in a FORTRAN-level language, called APT, cf. ANSI X3.37-1977 /3/. APT programs are not only used to specify the path which the cutting tool is to traverse, but also the rate of the traversal and a variety of auxiliary operations, such as adjusting the flow of coolants during machining.

Second, since parts are designed to specific engineering tolerances, the position and orientation of the part throughout the manufacturing must be precisely determined. This is accomplished by fastening the part in a suitably designed fixture, such as a vise. Workholding fixtures may be mounted on one or more pallets, which are shuttled into proper position for either fixturing the part or presenting the part for machining.

Third, all of the implied transfers of material within an automated workstation are carried out by a programmable industrial robot, cf. Edkins /8/.

A fully automated manufacturing workstation is one whose resident capital equipment can be quickly re-configured to produce a large number of different manufacturing parts. This degree of flexibility has much in common with the manual manufacturing regime. In manual manufacture, workpieces are under the supervisory control of skilled human workers, who are routinely able to make very accurate judgments about such features as the linearity of the part's edges or the relative alignment of holes without special training. Human workers also bring an enormous store of commonsense knowledge, including sophisticated error-recovery procedures for repairing slightly damaged parts and returning the process to acceptable control bounds. Since there is little to recommend a flexible manufacturing system which consistently produces a large number of parts to obtain a few that pass muster, any economically viable FMS must be held within very tight control bounds, whose width depends upon such matters as the tolerances on the finished parts. That is, the control bounds must be shifted much closer to the nominal line than would be the case if the parts were being manufactured in the manual manufacturing regime. Hence, automated workstations must be able to monitor their own operating states and have the ability to adapt to their current environment.

3 The Design of AMPLE

Self-monitoring system must have access to internal representations of all of the entities whose behavior is to be controlled. Internal representations of this kind are called *world models*.

AMPLE may be pictured as a loosely bundled, extensible collection of software modules, distributed around a central nucleus, called *AMPLE/core*, whose primary function is to maintain the world model (Figure 1). As discussed in Section 4, the design of *AMPLE/core* is based on a few carefully chosen abstractions.

The design of the surrounding collection of modules, hereafter called *AMPLE/mod*, is harder to characterize. Membership in *AMPLE/mod* is decided by the functional requirements which the specific implementation of *AMPLE* is designed to satisfy. Some modules, such as those which provide disciplined access to *AMPLE/core*, will be required by all implementations. Others, such as those which support specific modes of interaction with the external environment, are usually tailored to their function; and thus, have a narrower scope.

The configuration of *AMPLE/mod* for the Version 0.1 Prototype are described in Section 5. In this implementation, *AMPLE* support two different kinds of external interface, allowing *AMPLE* to be used both as an off-line programming system and as a run-time support system within AMRF. As configured for the December 1986 AMRF test run, the Prototype implementation provided run-time support for the horizontal workstation (HWS) and the turning workstation (TWS), and off-line programming for HWS. (Figure 1)

4 AMPLE/core

The function of *AMPLE/core* is to maintain formally precise representations of all physical objects and processes in the manufacturing domain:

- *parts*, including representations for geometric attributes, topological attributes, tolerance and dimensioning data, and administrative data;

- *devices*, including NC-machines, fixtures and specialized workholding devices, NC-machine tools and tool-changing devices, robots, grippers and other end-effectors;

- *sensors*, which may either be atomic sensors, such as contact switches, or more complicated sensory systems consisting of a network of simpler sensors; and

- *processes*, which are associated with manufacturing devices and provide the methods for bringing about physical changes in the workstation or the manufactured part.

The construction of world models poses many difficult conceptual problems. The basic problem is the invention of techniques that are powerful enough to allow all necessary information to be represented, and yet simple enough to allow users to readily grasp the general structural details. Though this problem obviously has no unique solution, the strategy adopted in *AMPLE* is to associate each type of entity to be represented with a *generic template*.

A template is a structural hypothesis that identifies those features of devices that are essential. For example, devices differ from one another in complicated ways, but considered abstractly, a device can be defined as any entity that (i) has finitely many components each of which is itself a device, (ii) has the capability to perform a finite, but extensible, set of operations, and (iii) occupies one of a finite number of states. Definitions of this sort can be expressed by an abstract type definition:

```
typedef ≺device-type-name≻ is device

    components are
        ≺component-list≻
    end components;
    operations are
```

3

```
    ≺operation-list≻
    end operations;
    states are
      ≺state-list≻
    end states;
  end device;
```

There are many different kinds of programmable devices in any workstation. To achieve the widest degree of flexibility and portability, equipment interfaces should be considered as links between abstract device specifications in the type definition and equipment-dependent device drivers. Since the primary mechanism for device abstraction is the specification of an operation list, each component of which consist of a single *main verb*, followed by zero or more *qualifying phrases*, the link between *AMPLE*-level commands and equipment-level control programs can be established by instantiating an equipment-level template, written in whatever that equipment recognizes as its native language. For a more thorough discussion of the issues involved in the use of such templates, see Boudreaux /5/ and /6/.

4.1 Core Support Modules

Given the central importance of the world models, a great deal of effort has been devoted to the organization of those software tools that are used to allow the user to have access to them.

4.1.1 Workspace Manager (WM)

To encourage disciplined access to symbolic names in *AMPLE* the Version 0.1 *AMPLE/mod* Prototype uses workspace management system. A workspace is a collection of symbolic names. Upon entering a workspace, users are permitted access to its resident names, and also acquire certain rights to add, delete, or otherwise modify them. Upon exiting the workspace, access to its names – and hence all other rights – are automatically revoked.

4.1.2 Lexical Analyser (Lexx)

Because of the specialized requirements of industrial control, and especially the requirement that *AMPLE* cause potentially dangerous physical motions, certain classes of users must be able to tailor the system to their own needs. *Lexx* is a module which provides such users with methods for introducing new symbolic names that have pre-defined meaning in the application domain and for assigning them formal definitions in *AMPLE*.

4.1.3 Object-oriented EDitor (OED)

To ensure that objects in *AMPLE/core* are processed in a disciplined way, all changes to them are made through a special module, called the *Object-oriented EDitor (OED)*. *OED* is a syntax-directed editor which initially understands the characteristic structure of LISP objects, and which can be taught to recognize the structure of *AMPLE* values which are generated with the *Lexx* module.

4

5   AMPLE/mod

Other *AMPLE/mod* modules allow the programmer to selectively examine different parts of the *AMPLE* environment, in much the same manner that operating system commands allow users to examine the available directories, to get assistance by invoking HELP commands, and to control any one of a number of well-defined, but extensible, computational processes. Though *AMPLE* has been designed to be an extensible system, it will clarify the intended mode of operation if some of the external modules in Version 0.1 are described in more detail.

5.1   User Interface

When operating as an off-line programming system, workstations programmers may select the operations to be performed by mousepicks from a user-defined menu, and also by responding appropriately when questioned for additional information.

5.2   Communication Package (Acomm)

When operating in real-time support mode, the communication link with HWS and TWS is supplied by this module. Though several different kinds of data can be transmitted, the most important information is contained in process plans.

5.3   Process Planning Interface (APPI)

The purpose of this module is to parse process plans, once they have been made available, and to determine that the process plans are correct and complete.

A process plan is correct if the following conditions are satisfied: the plan is syntactically correct and agrees with the AMRF flat file format for process plans; and all of the workelements defined in the plan can be performed by the targeted workstation.

A process plan is complete if all workelements needed to manufacture the part have been provided in the proper sequence. If the plan is incomplete, the verifier will identify the missing element by issuing either an "ERROR, MISSING ELEMENT" message or an appropriate "WARNING" if the missing element is not critical. In either case, the user may then decide whether to correct the condition or pass the plan on, with notes, to the part programmer.

5.4   Real-Time Control Interface (ARTCI)

This module accepts high-level instructions, either interactively from the user interface or remotely from APPI, and then generates equipment-level control data, and data to drive the animation package. Equipment-level control data is highly machine dependent, and thus cannot be transported from one controller to another. One primary motivation for the design of ARTCI is to encourage high-level process abstraction.

5.5   Workstation Animation Package (AWAP)

This module accepts input from ARTCI and generates a fully animated preview of the all of the physical motions that the associated control data, if actually executed, would produce. In this manner, AWAP allows off-line validation and testing of control programs.

To enhance the accuracy and reliability of AWAP, all motions are based on kinematic models of the moving components. For example, the kinematic model for the robots will not allow any motion during which joint angle limits are violated.

5.6 NC Verification Package (NCVer)

Part programming is the procedure whereby the sequence of elemental operations to be performed by a numerically controlled (NC) machine are specified and documented. The purpose of this module is to verify that NC part programs, as expressed in Cutter Location files (CLfiles) in the programming language APT /3/, are correct before they are actually used.

NCVer first screens the APT CLfile to determine that it is free of gross errors, i.e., checking COOLANT ON before any cutting operation is performed, and second determines whether a part program can produce the desired shape from an initial stock item or in-process part. The verifier is integrated with the part programming system to provide the user with an interactive, graphics-based system. Specifically, the verifier uses a solid model of the finished and in-process parts as well as models of cutting tools, fixtures, and the machine tool itself to provide visual and analytic verification of CLfiles. The verifier detects overcuts, undercuts, and collisions of the cutter or spindle with fixture elements.

6 Work in Progress

Since the beginning of the *AMPLE* project in October 1984, the focus of our effort has been on the the generation of control data and its off-line verification. Though additional work in this direction is still needed, our focus in the near future will be devoted to the the extension of *AMPLE/mod*. To better support the needs of the manufacturing community, which already depends quite heavily on commercially available CAD/CAM tools, some controlled tests will be done to determine the degree of effort required to fit pre-existent modules into *AMPLE/mod*. Some work in this direction has already been done, most notably, the very early partial integration of ICM's Geometric Solid Modeler (GMS) in the Prototype implementation, but more such co-operative efforts need to be undertaken to convincingly establish the adequacy of the *AMPLE* methodology.

Though many possible additions to *AMPLE/mod* could be undertaken, one that seems especially worthy is the *AMPLE Part Window*. The design of the Part Window will be based on the representation of parts in the current IGES standard /9/ and will be extended to incorporate other product data information as that becomes available through the on-going Product Data Exchange Specification (PDES) effort.

Part geometry data provide the information necessary to characterize the geometry of the part in a computer-readable form. In the initial stage, part geometry data will be represented using wireframe information structures, whose formats are described in IGES, Version 3.0. The defining characteristic of wireframe systems is that the geometry of parts is represented by points, lines, curves, circles, and so on. More complicated geometric features are described by splicing together simpler features or by introducing spline functions, i.e., piecewise continuous polynominal interpolation functions. In subsequent stages, more advanced geometric representations, including boundary representations and geometric solids, will be undertaken. During this phase of the construction of the Part Window, some careful thought will have to be given to the issue of the the *rational segmentation* of part features. Some preliminary work in this direction has already been undertaken by CAM-I, see /7/.

To be useful in the manufacturing process, a representation of part geometry must be accompanied by representations of dimensioning data. These data give information about the magnitude, or size, of specific features of the part so that all sizes and shapes can be determined without assuming the magnitude of any unrepresented dimensions. Since it is not possible to produce exact dimensions, tolerancing data must also be included. Conventional tolerances may be expressed as allowable errors on the dimension, e.g., 1.00 ± 0.05 mm specifies a dimensional variation which is constrained to lie in the interval 0.95 to 1.05 mm. Methods for minimizing cumulative error in dimensional tolerances are described in ANSI Y14.5M-1982

Manufactured parts must have some determinate properties and attributes which allow them to perform the specific function for which they were designed. This is true of manufactured parts which have been designed to fit within larger units, like gears and other single-block pieces, and also for such large-scale assemblies as airplanes and nuclear reactors, which may be among the most complicated entities ever designed. In order to guarantee that the product will indeed do its job, we must have a clear statement of part specifications, including the dimensioning scheme for the part, and also a description of permitted variations, which are given as tolerances.

The specifications of a part may be thought of as a complicated property, expressed in a formal language such as the first-order logic, which the part either satisfies or does not satisfy. In this case, specifications may be represented as Boolean gates through which the part either passes or fails to pass. This account assumes that the specifications are well-enough defined that those parts that pass will perform up to – and maybe slightly beyond – the demands placed upon them through their active worklife in the final assembled product.

Bibliography

1. Albus, J.S. *Brains, Behavior, and Robotics.* McGraw-Hill; 1981.

2. Albus, J.S., Barbera, A.J., Nagel, R.N. "Theory and Practice of Hierarchical Control," *23rd IEEE Computer Society International Conference*, September 1981, 18-39.

3. ANSI X3.37-1977, "Programming Language APT," American National Standards Institute, Inc.; 1977.

4. ANSI Y14.5M-1982, "Dimensioning and Tolerancing," The American Society of Mechanical Engineers; 1983.

5. Boudreaux, J.C. "Problem Solving and the Evolution of Programming Languages," *The Role of Language in Problem Solving-1*, edited by R. Jernigan, B.W. Hamill, and D.M. Weintraub, North-Holland, 1985; 103-126.

6. Boudreaux, J.C. "AMPLE: A Programming Language Environment for Automated Manufacturing," *The Role of Language in Problem Solving - 2*; edited by J.C. Boudreaux, B. Hamill, and R. Jernigan, North Holland, Amsterdam, 1986.

7. "CAM-I's Illustrated Glossary of Workpiece Form Features," Computer Aided Manufacturing-International, Inc., Arlington, TX; R-80-PPP-02.1, revised May 1981.

8. Edkins, M. "Linking industrial robots and machine tools," in A. Pugh, *Robotic Technology*, Peregrinus; 1983.

9. Smith, B.M. and Wellington, J. "Initial Graphics Exchange Specification (IGES)," Version 3.0, U.S. Department of Commerce, National Bureau of Standards, NBSIR 86-3359, April 1986.

10. Wilensky, R. *LISPcraft*, W.W. Norton; 1984.

AMPLE Flow Diagram

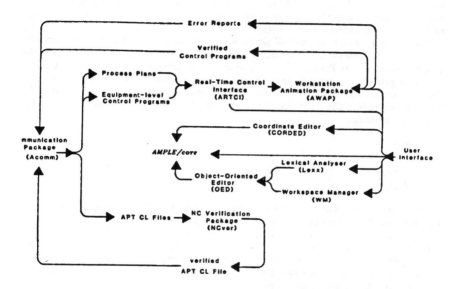

Figure 1. Schematic of the *AMPLE* Version 0.1 Prototype

Appendix: LISP and AMPLE/Core

Dialects of LISP have been the primary tools in the field of artificial intelligence almost from the beginning. However, the idea that this family of languages should be considered for applications outside of this field is an idea that until very recently would not have been seriously entertained. In this section, I will briefly explain FranzLISP, which is the LISP dialect actually used as the conceptual paradigm for *AMPLE/core*. For a more thorough examination of the ideas sketched here, see /5/.

One feature which runs through almost all dialects of LISP is that it is an interactive language which presents the user with a comparatively simple interface. Thus, from the user's perspective, the FranzLISP system consists of an interpreter which signals its availability by printing a prompt symbol. When the user responds by keying in an expression, the interpreter immediately returns the value of that expression on the next line. The following example is the transcript of two very simple exchanges between a user and the FranzLISP system:

```
-> 12
12
-> 23.4567
23.4567
```

In this case, the user has keyed in an integer value, which in FranzLISP jargon is called a fixnum, and then a floating point number, or flonum.

FranzLISP recognizes only two kinds of objects: atoms and lists. Atoms include such scalar values as integers, floating point reals, symbols, and strings. A list is an object that may always be resolved into a head component which may either an atom or a list, and a tail component which must be a list. The accepted notation for lists is to enclose their components within mated parentheses:

$$(A \ B)$$

In this example, the head is the symbolic atom **A**, and the tail is the list **(B)**. The list which has no components is called the null list and may be represented by the empty-nest expression "()" or by the constant symbol "nil". The null list is a useful artifact, especially in that it permits us to disambiguate such expressions as **(B)**, which is the list whose head is the symbol **B** and whose tail is the null list.

The only other class of entities recognized by FranzLISP are functions. In order to signal the FranzLISP interpreter that a particular function is to be applied to a (possibly empty) sequence of arguments, the programmer simply presents the interpreter with a list object whose head is the symbolic name of the function and whose tail is the list of the expressions to be passed to the function as arguments.

Two functions, **car** and **cdr**, are used to select the components of any list; in particular, car selects the head component and cdr selects the tail:

```
-> (car '(A B))
A
-> (cdr '(A B))
(B)
```

10

e single quote is an important FranzLISP function which is used to signal the FranzLISP erpreter that the FranzLISP object following the occurrence of the single quote is not be evaluated but treated as a literal. There are several important contexts in which the gle quote function is used covertly, for example, the FranzLISP function **setq**, which breviates *set quote*, is used to assign FranzLISP values to symbols:

```
-> (setq ab '(A B))
(A B)
```

he effect of the evaluation of this function is the association of the value of the second gument with the symbol in the initial argument place. This symbol may then be used as FranzLISP variable. The variable **ab** and its current value is stored in otherwise hidden mbol table, and from this point on, if the interpreter is presented with this name, it will spond with the assigned value:

```
-> ab
(A B)
```

here is one primitive constructor function for lists, namely, **cons**, which when applied to wo arguments, returns a list whose head is equal to the first argument and whose tail is qual to the second:

```
-> (cons 'A '(B))
(A B)
```

ymbols may also be used to represent entities with properties, where the property name is itself a symbol and the value of the property is any FranzLISP expression. Thus, to express the fact that bee is the **name-of** B, we would execute:

```
-> (putprop 'B 'bee 'name-of)
bee
```

To retrieve the value of a property, we would write

```
-> (get 'B 'name-of)
bee
```

All FranzLISP systems share the characteristic that programmers are encouraged to construct new application-specific functions of their own devising. Once written, these functions have the same status as the functions supplied by the FranzLISP system. To illustrate this important feature, let's use the example of the square function:

```
-> (def square (lambda (X) (times X X)))
square
```

The response square tells us that the function is subsequently available as a FranzLISP function, as the following exchanges clearly indicate:

```
-> (square 4)
16
-> (square 2.36)
5.5696
```

11

Note that **def** is just another FranzLISP function, differing from others that have already been mentioned, primarily with respect to its side effects on the FranzLISP environment. Like **setq**, this function causes a value to be associated with a symbolic name, in this case the symbolic name **square**. It associates this symbol with the otherwise anonymous function defined by the lambda abstraction formula

$$(\text{lambda } (X) \text{ (times } X \ X))$$

The variable X in this definition is said to be *lambda bound*, which means that the actual value is dependent upon the argument being passed during the activation of the function. In effect, the lambda expression creates a nested environment in which all lambda bound variables are set to the argument values, then the inner expression is evaluated in the usual way until some resulting value emerges. Once this value has been obtained, the nested environment is deleted and the resulting value is returned in place.

Every FranzLISP variable ranges over the entire domain of LISP values. That is, FranzLISP only recognizes universal typefree variables. Of course, the fact that LISP is not strongly typed does not mean that there is no way in LISP to enforce the underlying discipline, which is useful in many practical contexts. In LISP, as in set theory, one considers types to be predicates, that is, suitably defined Boolean-valued functions which return the value t if the argument is a bonafide member of the type, and **nil** otherwise. The following definition introduces the type predicate **natural**:

```
(def natural (lambda (intx)
    (and (fixp intx) (not (lessp intx 0)))))
```

The monadic function **fixp** returns **t** if its argument is an integer.

There are advantages to be had by accepting the *types-as-predicates* approach which are difficult or impossible to simulate in strongly typed languages, for example:

```
(def even (lambda (intx)
    (and (natural intx) (equal (mod intx 2) 0))))
(def odd (lambda (intx)
    (and (natural intx) (equal (mod intx 2) 1))))
```

Though not particularly interesting in their own right, these definitions do show that type names can be associated with infinitely large collections of LISP objects.

To achieve the effect of abstract data types in *AMPLE/core*, one approach is to stipulate some formal mechanism for collecting together and then associating a symbolic name with a class of structurally similar lists. The simplest way to define such a typing mechanism is to select a few type *constructors*, say **enumeration**, **record**, and **array**, but then to leave open the possibility of eventually adding to this list.

Suppose, for example, we wanted to define a type **POINT**, then we would probably want to construct a list whose display-form is:

```
typedef POINT is
    record
        X-ord : float;
        Y-ord : float;
        Name : string;
    end record;
```

12

In this case, we are using the **record** constructor. Since every record is a finite sequence of fields, each of which has a field name and a correpsonding type, one obvious FranzLISP object which seems to express the same information as definition of **POINT** is

$$((\text{X-ord float})(\text{Y-ord float})(\text{Name string}))$$

A very nice feature of this representation is that we can move from one field specification to the next by simply **cdr**-ing down the list, and then **car**-ing the resulting value. Once we have grasped a field specification, then one application of **car** will yield the field name, and one application of **cadr** will yield the field type.

But the selection of this representation is not enough. We also need to associate the field sequence with the type name **POINT**, and we also have to keep in mind that **POINT** was defined by using the **record** mechanism. One way to do this, though by no means the only way, is to use the **putprop** function:

```
(putprop 'RECORD
        '((X-ord float)(Y-ord float)(Name string))
        'POINT)
```

which has the effect of putting the record's fields on the property list of the atom **'RECORD** under the indicator **'POINT**. If this is done, then the *AMPLE* definition of **POINT** could be obtained as follows:

$$(\text{get 'RECORD 'POINT})$$

Since property lists are always extendable by the easy process of **putprop**-ing under a new symbolic indicator, this approach is a completely general method for building records in FranzLISP.

The techniques for other *AMPLE/core* representations may be handled in an analogous fashion. Thus, the job of finding a representation for the **enumeration** constructor is very simple indeed. Suppose we consider the type **BOOLEAN**:

$$\text{typedef BOOLEAN is (true false);}$$

then the only reasonable approach is to associate the list of values with the type name by **putprop**-ing on the special symbol **'ENUMERATION**. In order to achieve a good fit with FranzLISP, we should also establish a link between the value **'false** and **nil**, and **'true** and t, since the second components are the Booleans of FranzLISP.

4. TITLE AND SUBTITLE

The AMPLE Project

6. PERFORMING ORGANIZATION *(If joint or other than NBS, see Instructions)*

NATIONAL BUREAU OF STANDARDS
DEPARTMENT OF COMMERCE
WASHINGTON, D.C. 20234

9. SPONSORING ORGANIZATION NAME AND COMPLETE ADDRESS *(Street, City, State, ZIP)*

10. SUPPLEMENTARY NOTES

☐ Document describes a computer program; SF–185, FIPS Software Summary, is attached.

11. ABSTRACT *(A 200-word or less factual summary of most significant information. If document includes a significan bibliography or literature survey, mention it here)*

This report describes the Automated Manufacturing Programming Language Environ (AMPLE) system, being developed within the Center for Manufacturing Engineerin the National Bureau of Standards. The development of this system is being und to provide a precise, conceptually transparent medium for the construction of control interfaces to industrial processes; and to address the technical and e requirements of small-batch flexible manufacturing systems.

13. AVAILABILITY

☒ Unlimited
☐ For Official Distribution. Do Not Release to NTIS
☐ Order From Superintendent of Documents, U.S. Government Printing Office, Washington, D.C. 20402.

☒ Order From National Technical Information Service (NTIS), Springfield, VA. 22161

CPSIA information can be obtained
at www.ICGtesting.com
Printed in the USA
BVHW070837140119
537774BV00029B/2400/P